CONVECTION OVEN COOKBOOK

Delicious and Easy-to-Cook Countertop Convection Oven Recipes for Beginners

Kathleen Nolove

© Copyright 2021 by _____Kathleen Nolove_____ - All rights reserved.

The following Book is reproduced below with the goal of providing information that is as accurate and reliable as possible. Regardless, purchasing this Book can be seen as consent to the fact that both the publisher and the author of this book are in no way experts on the topics discussed within and that any recommendations or suggestions that are made herein are for entertainment purposes only. Professionals should be consulted as needed prior to undertaking any of the action endorsed herein.

This declaration is deemed fair and valid by both the American Bar Association and the Committee of Publishers Association and is legally binding throughout the United States.

Furthermore, the transmission, duplication, or reproduction of any of the following work including specific information will be considered an illegal act irrespective of if it is done electronically or in print. This extends to creating a secondary or tertiary copy of the work or a recorded copy and is only allowed with the express written consent from the Publisher. All additional right reserved.

The information in the following pages is broadly considered a truthful and accurate account of facts and as such, any inattention, use, or misuse of the information in question by the reader will render any resulting actions solely under their purview. There are no scenarios in which the publisher or the original author of this work can be in any fashion deemed liable for any hardship or damages that may befall them after undertaking information described herein.

Additionally, the information in the following pages is intended only for informational purposes and should thus be thought of as universal. As befitting its nature, it is presented without assurance regarding its prolonged validity or interim quality. Trademarks that are mentioned are done without written consent and can in no way be considered an endorsement from the trademark holder.

Table of Content

INTRODUCTION 7

BREAKFAST 11
- Roasted Brussels Sprouts 12
- Cowboy Quiche 14
- Scrambled Eggs 16
- Grilled Cheese Sandwich 18
- Hard-Boiled Eggs 20
- Apple Breakfast Bread 21
- Baked Oatmeal 23

APPETIZERS & SNACKS 25
- Sweet Potato Fries 26
- Margherita Pizza 28
- Avocado Fries 30

VEGETABLES 33
- Roasted Cauliflower, Olives, and Chickpeas 34
- Fruit and Vegetable Skewers 35
- Roasted Sweet Potatoes With Rosemary 37
- Tangy Roasted Broccoli With Garlic 39
- Roasted Carrots With Garlic 40
- Savory Roasted Balsamic Vegetables 42

SEAFOOD 43
- Scallops and Spring Veggies 44
- Beer-Battered Fish and Chips 46
- Fried Calamari 48
- Panko-Crusted Tilapia 49
- Snapper Scampi 51
- Fish Tacos 52
- Juicy Citrus Baked Salmon 54

POULTRY 57
- Chicken Roast With Pineapple Salsa 58
- Cheese Stuffed Chicken 59
- Orange Curried Chicken Stir-Fry 61
- Fried Chicken 63
- Southern Fried Chicken 65
- Chicken Tenders 67

- Salt and Pepper Chicken Wings 69
- Garlic Herb Butter Roast Chicken 71
- Seasoned Chicken 73

MEAT 75

- Meatloaf 76
- Swedish Meatballs 78
- Pork Belly 80
- Roast Lamb 82

BREAD 83

- Four Cheese Margherita Pizza 84
- Satay Chicken Pizza 86
- Black and White Pizza 87
- Bread Machine Bagels 89
- Bagel and Cheese Bake 91

CAKE & DESSERT 93

- Single-Serving Chocolate Chip Cookies 94
- Strawberry Chocolate Chip Banana Bread Bars 96
- Lemon Shortbread 98
- Carrot Cake Cookies 100
- Homemade Fudgy Brownies 102
- Teriyaki Sauce 105
- Poppy Seed Pound Cake 107
- Apple-Toffee Upside-Down Cake 109
- Chocolate Nut Brownies 111

MEASUREMENT CONVERSION CHART 113

INTRODUCTION

Have you heard of an oven? This heating mechanism is a great alternative to the traditional heaters, especially for your kitchen. Convection ovens are smaller compared to the conventional ones. This is because their air movement technology has lessened the need for large ceiling areas. Unlike the conventional ones, these are specially designed with a fan that circulates the air inside it. This mode of heating is the most efficient one that has been developed to date. This can be considered a much better option than the conventional ovens. You must have heard the term 'low calorie', however, ovens do not have low-calorie features but they do manage to consume less amount of power.

Convection ovens cook almost six times faster than the normal stoves, and not only does it reduce the cooking time, it also enhances the flavors of the food. These ovens though small, are technically advanced. The technology used in ovens is the same one that is used on commercial airplanes to heat them. The convection heating system's efficiency is highly dependent on the recipes used by the user. Of course, the user has complete control over the level of heating and the features of the oven. The specialty of an oven is that it starts cooking the food from the top and the bottom surfaces and not just the top. This gives not only the extra flavors but also prevents the disasters like the burning of food as it keeps the food evenly warmed. This is another great advantage of an oven. However, it is important to correctly follow the instructions given when purchasing these ovens. Convection ovens are great for people who wish to cook in bulk. This depends on the user's characteristics. Small households may cook on a regular basis, but someone who is fond of baking cookies or enjoying baking bread will require an oven. This type of oven is also suited for people who wish to use it for heating green stuff, for instance, for the use of a steamer. Another great advantage of this oven is that it can be used for cooking a whole meal. If the oven is of good quality, the dish can be cooked perfectly well and does not have the starchy taste or the burnt taste that is common with traditionally cooked food. The cooking process on this oven is much faster than other ceramic or traditional stoves. You should also note that this is significantly more energy efficient as it does not require more energy consumption than other types of stoves.

The oven is best suited for those people who feel that they would like to cook in huge batches of food. The choice of an oven depends on the intended use of the oven. You should choose the right oven for a particular purpose. Another advantage of the oven is that it makes the food come out perfectly by nourishing the food with liquid. This in no way requires you to thaw the frozen food in the traditional oven if you have frozen food for your oven. Of course, you should not cook frozen food on a normal heating device as it may turn hazardous.

In order to have the best out of your oven, you should follow the instructions to a T for safety measures. Before you purchase the convection oven, ensure that it is of a good quality. Ensure that the oven heats evenly. Also, ensure that it operates without making too much noise. It should also be very convenient for storage of the food. It should also be easy to clean.

Different Types of Convection Oven

There are several types of Convection Ovens; the most common types are divided into two categories. The first type is differentiated by the placement of the fan and additional heating element; this is the regular and the true convection oven.

The second type is classified by its placement or position in the kitchen; the major types are the countertop convection ovens and the floor models.

Regular convection oven

A regular convection oven is a device used to heat various types of food and beverages. A convection oven possesses several 'products' for delivering heat to the food placed in the oven.

True convection oven

A true convection oven is a natural method of cooking that is used in most restaurants. The cost of running a true convection oven is virtually nothing because they cut out the expensive internal electric or gas-powered convection fan, called a blower, which costs over $400 to replace. The idea behind the true convection oven is to use the air patterns that are naturally produced during cooking to distribute heat evenly to all areas of the oven.

Countertop convection oven

A countertop convection oven is like a countertop microwave. Instead of microwaves, it sends the hot air around and cooks the food from convection. And it has a door for the steam to get out.

Floor model convection oven

A floor model convection oven is a thing to envy. It's large enough to hold a 13"x9" cake tin, or the 8"x8" pan I use to bake brownies. The convection fan hubbub its blades mounted at the top of the dome-shaped door to mix the warm air as it cooks your meal.

It's a solid iron machine that makes my brownies with a crackling sound.

Breakfast

Roasted Brussels Sprouts

Preparation time: 30 minutes

Cooking time: 20 minutes

Servings: 4

INGREDIENTS:

- 2 lbs. Brussels Sprouts, cut
- 1/4 cup olive oil
- Fresh lemon juice
- 1 teaspoon minced fresh sage
- 2 tablespoon mixed seasonal Herbs
- Salt and Pepper
- 1/4 cup Pine nuts
- 1/4 cup freshly minced Parmesan-Reggiano

DIRECTIONS:

1. Preheat the oven to 204°C or 400°F.

2. Coat the Brussels sprouts with all the ingredients evenly in a plastic bag.

3. Put the Brussels sprouts inside a huge sheet pan.

4. Roast for 10 minutes inside the oven. Put cheese, pine nuts, and some lemon juice afterward.

NUTRITION:

- Calories: 135
- Carbs: 11g
- Protein: 3.9g
- Fat: 9.8g.

Cowboy Quiche

Preparation time: 35 minutes

Cooking time: 55 minutes

Servings: 8

INGREDIENTS:

- 1 red potato with sliced skin (keep it short)
- 1 onion, minced
- 1/2 jalapeno with minced seeds
- 1 stick butter, melted
- 1 teaspoon salt
- Black pepper
- 10 white mushrooms, minced
- 5-7 bacon strips
- 1/2 cup sliced ham
- 1/2 red pepper, minced
- 1/2 green pepper, minced
- 1/4 cup grated Cheddar
- 1/4 cup grated Gruyere
- 6 eggs
- 12 ounces milk
- pint heavy cream
- 1 teaspoon ground nutmeg
- 2 unbaked (9-inch) pie doughs

DIRECTIONS:

1. Preheat the oven to 177°C or 350°F. Put the veggies on a parchment paper-filled tray.

2. Put some melted butter with salt and pepper over vegetables, and bake for 15 minutes.

3. Put mushrooms separately in a parchment paper-filled tray with melted butter on top. Cook for 5 minutes.

4. Cook bacon strips on a different tray until crisp.

5. Put minced ham inside the oven and cook everything properly.

6. Mix all the ingredients to blend properly.

7. Stir eggs, milk, and heavy cream separately, add some salt and black pepper with nutmeg and mix properly.

8. Add the ingredients in a pan containing raw crust with the egg mixture. Bake for 35 minutes.

NUTRITION:
- Calories: 257.9
- Carbs: 24g
- Protein: 11.6g
- Fat: 9g

Scrambled Eggs

Preparation time: 10 minutes

Cooking time: 5 minutes.

Servings: 2

INGREDIENTS:

- 1/2 tablespoon unsalted butter
- 2 big eggs
- 1 tablespoon water kosher salt
- Fresh ground pepper

DIRECTIONS:

1. Preheat the oven to 149°C or 300°F. Turn the fan on for circulation.

2. Put seasoned eggs on the lightly greased pan and cover with foil.

3. Cook for 5-10 minutes or until the eggs are set

4. Use a spatula to stir the eggs, and scrape the sides.

NUTRITION:
- Calories: 149
- Carbs: 1g
- Protein: 12g
- Fat: 6.7g.

Grilled Cheese Sandwich

Preparation time: 5 minutes

Cooking time: 10 minutes

Servings: 2

INGREDIENTS:

- 4 slices of sourdough bread
- 2 slices of cheddar cheese
- 2 tablespoons butter, unsalted, softened
- 2 slices of Havarti cheese

DIRECTIONS:

1. Turn on the oven, set the temperature to 375 degrees F, and then select the oven cooking method.

2. Meanwhile, spread the butter on one side of each bread slice and then place two bread slices butter-side-down on the oven tray.

3. Top the bread slices with 1 slice of Havarti and cheddar cheese, and then arrange the remaining bread slices on top of the cheese, butter-side up.

4. Place the oven tray into the oven and then cook for 7 minutes.

5. Flip the sandwiches, continue cooking them for 3 minutes until toasted on all sides, and then serve.

NUTRITION:
- Calories: 334
- Fat: 23g
- Carbs: 20g
- Protein: 13g
- Fiber: 2g

Hard-Boiled Eggs

Preparation time: 5 minutes

Cooking time: 15 minutes

Servings: 4

INGREDIENTS:

- 4 eggs

DIRECTIONS:

1. Turn on the oven, set the temperature to 270 degrees F, and then select the oven cooking method.
2. Meanwhile, place the eggs in the oven basket.
3. Then place the oven basket into the oven and cook for 15 minutes or more until hard-boiled.
4. When done, transfer the eggs into the bowl containing chilled water and let them soak for 10 minutes.
5. Peel the eggs, cut them into slices, and then serve.

NUTRITION:

- Calories: 155
- Fat: 11g
- Carbs: 1.1g
- Protein: 13g
- Fiber: 0g

Apple Breakfast Bread

Preparation time: 10 minutes

Cooking time: 1 hour

Servings: 8

INGREDIENTS:

- 2 medium apples, peeled, cored, chopped
- 2 cups all-purpose flour
- 1 teaspoon baking soda
- 1/2 teaspoon salt
- 1 cup of sugar
- 1 teaspoon ground cinnamon
- 1/2 teaspoon ground cloves
- 2 eggs
- 1/2 cup butter, unsalted

DIRECTIONS:

1. Turn on the oven, set the temperature to 350 degrees F, and then select the oven cooking method.

2. Meanwhile, place butter in a large bowl, beat in sugar until creamy and smooth, and then beat in eggs until blended.

3. Take a separate large bowl, add flour in it, add cinnamon, cloves, salt, and baking soda and then stir until mixed.

4. Stir the flour mixture into the butter mixture until moistened, and then fold in apple pieces.

5. Take an 8-by-4-inch loaf pan, grease it with butter, spoon the apple mixture in it and then bake for 1 hour until the top turn golden brown and inserted wooden toothpick comes out clean.

6. When done, let the bread cool in its pan for 15 minutes, then cool it completely on a wire rack and cut the bread into slices.

7. Serve straight away.

NUTRITION:

- Calories: 279
- Fat: 10.5g
- Carbs: 43.2g
- Protein: 4g
- Fiber: 1.5g

Baked Oatmeal

Preparation time: 5 minutes

Cooking time: 35 minutes

Servings: 9

INGREDIENTS:

- 1 1/2 cup mixed berries, fresh
- 3 cups oats, old-fashioned
- 1 teaspoon baking powder
- 1/4 teaspoon salt
- 1 teaspoon ground cinnamon
- 1/2 cup chopped walnuts
- 1 teaspoon vanilla extract, unsweetened
- 1/4 cup applesauce, unsweetened
- 1/2 cup maple syrup
- 1/4 cup butter, unsalted, melted, cooled
- 1 3/4 cups almond milk, unsweetened
- 2 eggs

DIRECTIONS:

1. Turn on the oven, set the temperature to 350 degrees F, and then select the oven cooking method.
2. Meanwhile, take a square baking dish, and then grease it with oil.
3. Take a large bowl, place all the ingredients in it except for nuts and then stir until combined.
4. Spoon the mixture into the prepared pan, sprinkle nuts on top and then bake for 35 minutes until set.
5. Serve straight away.

NUTRITION:

- Calories: 227
- Fat: 8g
- Carbs: 34g
- Protein: 5g
- Fiber: 4g

Appetizers & Snacks

Sweet Potato Fries

Preparation time: 5 minutes

Cooking time: 28 minutes

Servings: 4

INGREDIENTS:

- 2 sweet potatoes, about 6-ounces
- 1/4 teaspoon garlic powder
- 1/4 teaspoon of sea salt
- 1 teaspoon chopped thyme
- 1 tablespoon olive oil

DIRECTIONS:

1. Turn on the oven, set the temperature to 400 degrees F, and then select the oven cooking method.

2. Meanwhile, peel the potatoes and then cut them into 1/4-inch sticks.

3. Take a medium bowl, add garlic powder, salt, thyme, salt, and oil and then stir until combined.

4. Peel the sweet potatoes cut them into 1/4-inch sticks, add them to the oil mixture, and then toss until coated.

5. Spread the sweet potatoes on the oven basket in a single layer and then cook for 14 minutes until nicely browned, tossing halfway.

6. Repeat with the remaining sweet potato sticks and then serve.

NUTRITION:
- Calories: 104
- Fat: 3g
- Carbs: 17g
- Protein: 1g
- Fiber: 3g

Margherita Pizza

Preparation time: 5 minutes

Cooking time: 14 minutes

Servings: 4

INGREDIENTS:

- 1 pizza dough
- 1/4 cup basil leaves
- 1/2 cup pizza sauce
- 2 cups sliced mozzarella cheese
- 1/4 cup grated parmesan cheese

DIRECTIONS:

1. Turn on the oven, set the temperature to 475 degrees F, and then select the oven cooking method.

2. Meanwhile, transfer the pizza dough onto the clean working space dusted with flour and then roll it into a round shape.

3. Spread the pizza sauce on top, scatter mozzarella cheese on top and then sprinkle with parmesan cheese.

4. Transfer the prepared pizza to the baking pan and then bake for 14 minutes until the crust turns golden brown and the cheese turns golden.

5. When done, scatter basil leaves on top and then serve.

NUTRITION:

- Calories: 220
- Fat: 9g
- Carbs: 25g
- Protein: 11g
- Fiber: 1g

Avocado Fries

Preparation time: 5 minutes

Cooking time: 8 minutes

Servings: 4

INGREDIENTS:

- 2 avocados
- 1/2 cup all-purpose flour
- 1/2 cup panko breadcrumbs
- 1/4 teaspoon salt
- 1 1/2 teaspoon ground black pepper
- 2 eggs
- 1 tablespoon water

DIRECTIONS:

1. Turn on the oven, set the temperature to 400 degrees F, and then select the oven cooking method.
2. Meanwhile, place flour in a shallow dish and then stir in black pepper until mixed.
3. Crack the eggs in a separate shallow dish, add water and then whisk until combined.
4. Take a separate shallow dish and spread panko breadcrumbs in it.
5. Cut each avocado into eight wedges, dredge each avocado into flour, dip into the eggs and then coat in breadcrumb mixture.
6. Place prepared avocado wedges in the oven basket, spray with oil and then cook for 8 minutes, turning halfway.
7. When done, sprinkle salt over fries and then serve.

NUTRITION:

- Calories: 262
- Fat: 18g
- Carbs: 23g
- Protein: 5g
- Fiber: 7g

Vegetables

Roasted Cauliflower, Olives, and Chickpeas

Preparation time: 15 minutes

Cooking time: 24 minutes

Servings: 3

INGREDIENTS:

- 3 cup cauliflower florets
- 4 chopped garlic cloves
- 1/2 cup Spanish green olives
- 15 oz. chickpeas, rinsed and drained
- 1/4 tsp crushed red pepper
- 1 1/2 tablespoon olive oil
- 1 1/2 tablespoon parsley
- Salt taste

DIRECTIONS:

1. Place the cauliflower florets, garlic, Spanish green olives, chickpeas, crushed red pepper, parsley, and salt in a large bowl.
2. Pour oil over the ingredients, and then let it stand for about 2 to 3 minutes.
3. Toss until all the ingredients are well coated in the olive oil.
4. Place the olive oil coated ingredients at the bottom of a lined pan in a single even layer. Cook on 'HI' setting for about 22 to 24 minutes.
5. Serve hot with your preferred condiment on the side.

NUTRITION:

- Calories: 176
- Fat: 10.1g
- Protein: 4.2g
- Carbs: 17.6g

Fruit and Vegetable Skewers

Preparation time: 4 minutes

Cooking time: 16 minutes

Servings: 4

INGREDIENTS:

- 4 tablespoon virgin olive oil
- 3 tablespoon lemon juice
- 1 garlic clove, minced
- 2 tablespoon chopped parsley
- 1/2 teaspoon salt
- 1/2 teaspoon black pepper
- 1 sliced zucchini
- 1 sliced yellow squash
- 1/2 red bell pepper
- 1/2 cup cherry tomatoes

- 1/2 cup pineapple chunks
- 4 wooden skewers

DIRECTIONS:

1. In a large mixing bowl, combine olive oil, garlic, parsley, lemon juice, pepper, and salt. Pour into a large resalable plastic bag. Add zucchini, squash, bell pepper, and tomatoes. Seal bag shake to coat vegetables, and place in the refrigerator for a minimum of 1 hour
2. Remove vegetables from marinade and thread onto skewers, along with pineapple, alternating among each item.
3. Place skewers on the 4-inch rack. Cook on High Power (350 C) for 8 minutes.
4. Flip skewers over and cook for another 6-8 minutes until veggies are desired level of doneness.
5. Remove from the oven, transfer to a plate, and serve.

NUTRITION:

- Calories: 173
- Fat: 2.8g
- Carbs: 36.5g
- Protein: 5g

Roasted Sweet Potatoes With Rosemary

Preparation time: 15 minutes

Cooking time: 22 minutes

Servings: 4

INGREDIENTS:

- 1 1/2 pound sweet potatoes, cubed
- 1 teaspoon olive oil
- 1 dash chopped rosemary
- 1 dash lemon juice

DIRECTIONS:

1. In a bowl, toss sweet potatoes with oil. Evenly spread on the 10-inch baking sheet, sprinkle with rosemary. Place on 1-inch rack and back on High power (350 degrees F) for 12 minutes. Flip sweet potatoes over and cook an additional 10 minutes.
2. Drizzle with lemon juice and serve.

NUTRITION:

- Calories: 114
- Total Fat: 0g
- Carbs: 27g
- Protein: 2g

Tangy Roasted Broccoli With Garlic

Preparation time: 10 minutes

Cooking time: 17 minutes

Servings: 4

INGREDIENTS:

- 1 broccoli head
- 3 garlic cloves, minced
- 2 teaspoon virgin olive oil
- 1 teaspoon sea salt
- 1/2 teaspoon black pepper
- 1/2 teaspoon lemon juice

DIRECTIONS:

1. In a mixing bowl, add oil, salt, garlic and black pepper. Add broccoli. Mix to coat. Evenly scatter broccoli on the 10-inch baking sheet. Place on1-inch rack and roast on High power (350 degrees F) for about 10 minutes. Flip florets and cook another 5-7 minutes or until fork tender.
2. Plate and drizzle lemon juice. Serve at once.

NUTRITION:

- Calories: 141
- Carbs: 10g
- Fat: 10g
- Protein: 5g

Roasted Carrots With Garlic

Preparation time: 10 minutes

Cooking time: 20 minutes

Servings: 2

INGREDIENTS:

- 3 tablespoon olive oil
- 2 minced garlic cloves
- Sea salt, to taste
- 1-pound baby carrots

DIRECTIONS:

1. In a medium bowl, mix carrots with olive oil, salt, and garlic. Spread carrots in a single layer on a parchment or foil-lined baking sheet.

2. Place on 1-inch rack and cook on High power (350 F) for 15-20 minutes until carrots are tender.

NUTRITION:

- Calories: 95
- Fat: 6.9g
- Carbs: 7.6g
- Protein: 1g

Savory Roasted Balsamic Vegetables

Preparation time: 20 minutes

Cooking time: 30 minutes

Servings: 4

INGREDIENTS:

- 1 1/2 cup cubed butternut squash
- 1 cup chopped broccoli florets
- 1/2 chopped red onion
- 1 chopped zucchini
- 1 minced garlic clove
- 2 tablespoon virgin olive oil
- 1 1/2 teaspoon rosemary
- A pinch of salt, to taste
- 1 tablespoon balsamic vinegar

DIRECTIONS:

1. In a mixing bowl, add oil, rosemary, vinegar, pepper, and salt; mix to blend. Mix in the vegetables, mix to coat evenly.
2. Evenly spread on a parchment-lined baking sheet.
3. Place on 1-inch rack and cook on High power (350 degrees F) for about 15 minutes. Flip vegetables and cook for another 15 minutes or until squash is just softened.

NUTRITION:

- Calories: 148
- Fat: 4.6g
- Carbs: 25g
- Protein: 7g

Seafood

Scallops and Spring Veggies

Preparation time: 10 minutes

Cooking time: 8 minutes

Servings: 4

INGREDIENTS:

- 1/2 pound asparagus, ends trimmed, cut into 2-inch pieces
- 1 cup sugar snap peas
- 1 pound sea scallops
- 1 tablespoon lemon juice
- 2 teaspoons olive oil
- 1/2 teaspoon dried thyme
- Pinch salt
- Freshly ground black pepper

DIRECTIONS:

1. Place the asparagus and sugar snap peas in the oven basket.
2. Cook for 2 to 3 minutes or until the vegetables are just starting to get tender.
3. Meanwhile, check the scallops for a small muscle attached to the side, and pull it off and discard.
4. In a medium bowl, toss the scallops with the lemon juice, olive oil, thyme, salt, and pepper. Place into the oven basket on top of the vegetables.
5. Steam for 5 to 7 minutes, tossing the basket once during cooking time, until the scallops are just firm when tested with your finger and are opaque in the center, and the vegetables are tender. Serve immediately.

NUTRITION:

- Calories: 162
- Carbs: 10g
- Fat: 4g
- Protein: 22g
- Fiber: 3g

Beer-Battered Fish and Chips

Preparation time: 5 minutes

Cooking time: 30 minutes

Servings: 4

INGREDIENTS:

- 2 eggs
- 1 cup malty beer, such as Pabst Blue Ribbon
- 1 cup all-purpose flour
- 1/2 cup cornstarch
- 1 teaspoon garlic powder
- Salt
- Pepper
- Cooking oil
- (4-ounce) cod fillets

DIRECTIONS:

1. In a medium bowl, beat the eggs with the beer. In another medium bowl, combine the flour and cornstarch, and season with the garlic powder and salt and pepper to taste.
2. Spray the oven basket with cooking oil.
3. Dip each cod fillet in the flour and cornstarch mixture and then in the egg and beer mixture. Dip the cod in the flour and cornstarch a second time.
4. Place the cod in the oven. Do not stack. Cook in batches. Spray with cooking oil and cook for 8 minutes.
5. Open the oven and flip the cod. Cook for an additional 7 minutes.
6. Remove the cooked cod from the oven, then repeat steps 4 and 5 for the remaining fillets.
7. Serve with prepared fried frozen fries. Frozen fries will need to be cooked for 18 to 20 minutes at 400°F.
8. Cool before serving.

NUTRITION:

- Calories: 325
- Carbs: 41
- Fat: 4g
- Protein: 26g
- Fiber: 1g

Fried Calamari

Preparation time: 8 minutes

Cooking time: 7 minutes

Servings: 6-8

INGREDIENTS:

- 1/2 teaspoon salt
- 1/2 teaspoon Old Bay seasoning
- 1/3 cup plain cornmeal
- 1/2 cup semolina flour
- 1/2 cup almond flour
- 5-6 cup olive oil
- 1 1/2 pounds baby squid
- Pepper

DIRECTIONS:

1. Rinse squid in cold water and slice tentacles, keeping just 1/4-inch of the hood in one piece.
2. Combine 1-2 pinches of pepper, salt, Old Bay seasoning cornmeal, and both flours together. Dredge squid pieces into flour mixture and place into the oven basket.
3. Spray liberally with olive oil. Cook 15 minutes at 345 degrees till the coating turns a golden brown.

NUTRITION:

- Calories: 211
- Carbs: 55
- Fat: 6g
- Protein: 21g
- Sugar: 1g

Panko-Crusted Tilapia

Preparation time: 5 minutes

Cooking time: 10 minutes

Servings: 3

INGREDIENTS:

- 2 teaspoon Italian seasoning
- 2 teaspoon lemon pepper
- 1/3 cup panko breadcrumbs
- 1/3 cup egg whites
- 1/3 cup almond flour
- 3 tilapia fillets
- Olive oil

DIRECTIONS:

1. Place panko, egg whites, and flour into separate bowls. Mix lemon pepper and Italian seasoning in with breadcrumbs.

2. Pat tilapia fillets dry. Dredge in flour, then egg, then breadcrumb mixture.
3. Add to the oven basket and spray lightly with olive oil.
4. Cook 10-11 minutes at 400 degrees, making sure to flip halfway through cooking.

NUTRITION:
- Calories: 256
- Fat: 9g
- Protein: 39g
- Sugar: 5g

Snapper Scampi

Preparation time: 5 minutes

Cooking time: 10 minutes

Servings: 4

INGREDIENTS:

- 4 (6-ounce) skinless snapper or arctic char fillets
- 1 tablespoon olive oil
- 3 tablespoons lemon juice, divided
- 1/2 teaspoon dried basil
- Pinch salt
- Freshly ground black pepper
- 2 tablespoons butter
- 4 cloves garlic, minced

DIRECTIONS:

1. Rub the fish fillets with olive oil and 1 tablespoon of lemon juice. Sprinkle with the basil, salt, and pepper, and place in the oven basket.
2. Grill the fish for 7 to 8 minutes or until the fish just flakes when tested with a fork. Remove the fish from the basket and put it on a serving plate. Cover to keep warm. In a 6-by-6-by-2-inch pan, combine the butter, remaining 2 tablespoons lemon juice, and garlic Cook in the oven for 1 to 2 minutes or until the garlic is sizzling. Pour this mixture over the fish and serve.

NUTRITION:

- Calories: 265
- Carbs: 1g
- Fat: 11g
- Protein: 39g
- Fiber: 0g

Fish Tacos

Preparation time: 5 minutes

Cooking time: 15 minutes

Servings: 4

INGREDIENTS:

- 1 pound cod
- 1 tablespoon cumin
- 1/2 tablespoon chili powder
- 1 1/2 cup almond flour
- 1 1/2 cup coconut flour
- 10 ounces Mexican beer
- 2 eggs

DIRECTIONS:

1. Whisk beer and eggs together.
2. Whisk flours, pepper, salt, cumin, and chili powder together.

3. Slice cod into large pieces and coat in egg mixture, then flour mixture.
4. Spray the bottom of your oven basket with olive oil and add coated codpieces. Cook 15 minutes at 375 degrees.
5. Serve on lettuce leaves topped with homemade salsa.

NUTRITION:
- Calories: 178
- Carbs: 61g
- Fat: 10g
- Protein: 19g
- Sugar: 1g

Juicy Citrus Baked Salmon

Preparation time: 15 minutes

Cooking time: 20 minutes

Servings: 4

INGREDIENTS:

- 4 lemon slices
- 4 orange slices
- 4 salmon fillets
- A pinch salt and pepper to taste
- 2 tablespoon chopped dill
- 2 tablespoon sun-dried tomatoes
- 1 tablespoon extra-virgin olive oil
- 2/3 cup rice wine vinegar

DIRECTIONS:

1. Place lemon and orange slices, side by side, in the bottom of a shallow baking dish that will fit in a NuWave oven (10 x10). Place each salmon fillet across the citrus slices. Sprinkle with pepper and salt.
2. In a large mixing bowl, combine dill, sun-dried tomatoes, olive oil, and rice wine vinegar. Mix well, then drizzle mixture over salmon fillets.
3. Place on 1-inch rack and cook on High power (350 °C) for 7-8 minutes or till salmon is cooked through.
4. Serve and enjoy.

NUTRITION:

- Calories: 270
- Total Fat: 12.6g
- Total carbs: 5.4g
- Protein: 32.5g

Poultry

Chicken Roast With Pineapple Salsa

Preparation time: 10 minutes

Cooking time: 45 minutes

Servings: 2

INGREDIENTS:

- 1/4 cup extra virgin olive oil
- 1/4 cup freshly chopped cilantro
- 1 avocado, diced
- 1-pound boneless chicken breasts
- 2 cups canned pineapples
- 2 teaspoons honey
- Juice from 1 lime
- Salt and pepper to taste

DIRECTIONS:

1. Preheat the oven to 390°F.
2. Place the grill pan accessory in the oven.
3. Season the chicken breasts with lime juice, olive oil, honey, salt, and pepper.
4. Place on the grill pan and cook for 45 minutes.
5. Flip the chicken every 10 minutes to grill all sides evenly.
6. Once the chicken is cooked, serve with pineapples, cilantro, and avocado.

NUTRITION:

- Calories: 744
- Fat: 32.8g
- Protein: 4.7g
- Sugar: 5g

Cheese Stuffed Chicken

Preparation time: 5 minutes

Cooking time: 30 minutes

Servings: 4

INGREDIENTS:

- 1 tablespoon creole seasoning
- 1 tablespoon olive oil
- 1 teaspoon garlic powder
- 1 teaspoon onion powder
- 4 chicken breasts, butterflied and pounded
- 4 slices Colby cheese
- 4 slices pepper jack cheese

DIRECTIONS:

1. Preheat the oven to 390°F.
2. Place the grill pan accessory in the oven.

3. Create the dry rub by mixing in a bowl the creole seasoning, garlic powder, and onion powder. Season with salt and pepper if desired.
4. Rub the seasoning onto the chicken.
5. Place the chicken on a working surface and place a slice each of pepper jack and Colby cheese.
6. Fold the chicken and secure the edges with toothpicks.
7. Brush chicken with olive oil.
8. Grill for 30 minutes, and make sure to flip the meat every 10 minutes.

NUTRITION:
- Calories: 27
- Fat: 45.9g
- Protein: 73.1g
- Sugar: 0g

Orange Curried Chicken Stir-Fry

Preparation time: 10 minutes

Cooking time: 18 minutes

Servings: 4

INGREDIENTS:

- 3/4 pound boneless, skinless chicken thighs, cut into 1-inch pieces
- 1 yellow bell pepper, cut into 1 1/2-inch pieces
- 1 small red onion, sliced
- Olive oil for misting
- 1/4 cup chicken stock
- 2 tablespoons honey
- 1/4 cup orange juice
- 1 tablespoon cornstarch
- to 3 teaspoons curry powder

DIRECTIONS:

1. Put the chicken thighs, pepper, and red onion in the oven basket and mist with olive oil.
2. Cook for 12 to 14 minutes or until the chicken is cooked to 165°F, shaking the basket halfway through cooking time.
3. Remove the chicken and vegetables from the oven basket and set aside.
4. In a 6-inch metal bowl, combine the stock, honey, orange juice, cornstarch, and curry powder, and mix well. Add the chicken and vegetables, stir, and put the bowl in the basket.
5. Return the basket to the oven and cook for 2 minutes. Remove and stir, then cook for 2 to 3 minutes or until the sauce is thickened and bubbly.

NUTRITION:

- Calories: 230
- Fat: 7g
- Protein: 26g
- Fiber: 2g

Fried Chicken

Preparation time: 5 minutes

Cooking time: 20 minutes

Servings: 4

INGREDIENTS:

- 4 chicken thighs, with skin and bones
- 1/2 teaspoon salt
- 1/2 teaspoon ground black pepper

DIRECTIONS:

1. Turn on the oven, set the temperature to 350 degrees F, and then select the oven cooking method.

2. Meanwhile, season the chicken with salt and black pepper and then arrange them on the oven basket.

3. Then insert the fryer basket into the oven and bake the chicken for 10 minutes per side until cooked.

4. Serve straight away.

NUTRITION:

- Calories: 248
- Fat: 18g
- Carbs: 2g
- Protein: 18g
- Fiber: 0g

Southern Fried Chicken

Preparation time: 20 minutes

Cooking time: 18 minutes

Servings: 6

INGREDIENTS:

- 6 chicken legs
- 1 cup self-rising flour
- 1/4 cup cornstarch
- 2 eggs
- 1 tablespoon hot sauce
- 2 tablespoons buttermilk
- 1/4 cup of water
- For the Spice Mix:
- 1 1/2 teaspoon garlic powder
- 2 teaspoons sea salt
- 1 1/2 teaspoon ground black pepper
- 1 1/2 teaspoons paprika
- 1 teaspoon onion powder
- 1 teaspoon Italian seasoning

DIRECTIONS:

1. Turn on the oven, set the temperature to 350 degrees F, and then select the oven cooking method.
2. Meanwhile, take a small bowl, place the spice mix in it, and then stir until mixed.
3. Then sprinkle some of the spice mix on chicken legs and set aside until required.
4. Place flour in a large plastic bag add remaining spice mix and cornstarch and then stir until mixed.
5. Crack eggs in a large bowl, add hot sauce, pour water and milk, and then whisk until combined.
6. Place chicken legs in the flour mixture, seal the bag and then shake well until coated.
7. Arrange the chicken legs on a plate, let it rest for 5 minutes, coat each chicken leg in the egg mixture, and then coat in the flour mixture.
8. Let the coated chicken legs rest for 15 minutes, and then sprinkle with oil.
9. Arrange the chicken thighs on the oven basket and then cook for 9 minutes per side until golden brown.
10. When done, let the chicken rest for 5 minutes and then serve.

NUTRITION:

- Calories: 164
- Fat: 9g
- Carbs: 12g
- Protein: 20g
- Fiber: 3g

Chicken Tenders

Preparation time: 10 minutes

Cooking time: 22 minutes

Servings: 4

INGREDIENTS:

- 1 1/2 pound chicken breast tenders
- 1/4 cup flour
- 1/2 teaspoon seasoned salt
- 1 cup cornflake crumbs
- 1 cup breadcrumbs
- 1/2 teaspoon garlic powder
- 1 teaspoon paprika
- 1 teaspoon salt
- 1/2 teaspoon ground black pepper
- 2 eggs

- 2 tablespoons water

DIRECTIONS:

1. Turn on the oven, set the temperature to 425 degrees F, and then select the oven cooking method.

2. Meanwhile, cut the chicken tender into 3/4-inch pieces. Then season with salt and black pepper.

3. Place flour in a medium bowl, add salt, and then stir until mixed.

4. Place crumbs in a shallow dish, add salt, black pepper, garlic powder, and paprika and then stir until mixed.

5. Crack the eggs in a bowl and then whisk until blended.

6. Working on one chicken piece at a time, dredge it in flour, dip into eggs and then coat in breadcrumb mixture.

7. Place the coated chicken pieces on the baking pan, spray with oil and then bake for 18 to 22 minutes until thoroughly cooked.

8. Serve straight away.

NUTRITION:

- Calories: 527
- Fat: 8g
- Carbs: 67g
- Protein: 46g
- Fiber: 3g

Salt and Pepper Chicken Wings

Preparation time: 5 minutes

Cooking time: 45 minutes

Servings: 4

INGREDIENTS:

- 2 pounds of chicken wings
- 2 teaspoons sea salt
- 1 teaspoon ground black pepper
- 1 tablespoon chopped parsley
- 2 tablespoons olive oil

DIRECTIONS:

1. Turn on the oven, set the temperature to 425 degrees F, and then select the oven cooking method.

2. Meanwhile, place the chicken wings in a medium bowl, drizzle with oil and then toss well until coated.

3. Sprinkle salt and black pepper over the chicken wings and then toss well until coated.

4. Take a baking pan, line it with parchment paper, spread the chicken wings in a single layer, and then bake for 45 minutes until golden brown and crisp.

5. When done, sprinkle parsley over the chicken wings and then serve.

NUTRITION:
- Calories: 335
- Fat: 26g
- Carbs: 3g
- Protein: 22g
- Fiber: 1g

Garlic Herb Butter Roast Chicken

Preparation time: 10 minutes

Cooking time: 1 hour and 25 minutes

Servings: 4

INGREDIENTS:

- 4 pounds whole chicken, cleaned, rinsed
- 2 tablespoons minced garlic
- 1 medium head of garlic, peeled, cut in half crosswise
- 2 tablespoons chopped parsley
- 3 sprigs of rosemary
- 1 lemon, cut in half
- 2 teaspoons salt
- 2 teaspoons ground black pepper
- 1/4 cup unsalted butter, melted
- 3 tablespoons olive oil

DIRECTIONS:

1. Turn on the oven, set the temperature to 430 degrees F, and then select the oven cooking method.

2. Meanwhile, juice half of the lemon and then drizzle with butter and oil over the chicken, inside the cavity, and under the skin.

3. Season the chicken with salt and black pepper, and then sprinkle with parsley.

4. Rub the garlic over the chicken, then stuff rosemary and garlic head into the chicken cavity, squeeze the other lemon half, and tie the chicken legs with the kitchen twine.

5. Arrange the chicken on the baking pan, roast it for 1 hour and 20 minutes, baste it with juice, turn on the broiler and then broil the chicken for 3 minutes until golden brown.

6. When done, cover the chicken with foil, let it stand for 10 minutes, and then carve it into pieces.

7. Serve straight away.

NUTRITION:
- Calories: 510
- Fat: 31g
- Carbs: 4g
- Protein: 71g
- Fiber: 1g

Seasoned Chicken

Preparation time: 5 minutes

Cooking time: 35 minutes

Servings: 4

INGREDIENTS:

- 2 pounds chicken breasts, boneless, skinless
- 1 1/2 teaspoons dried parsley
- 1 teaspoon seasoned salt
- 1 teaspoon garlic powder
- 1 teaspoon dried basil
- 1 tablespoon olive oil

DIRECTIONS:

1. Turn on the oven, set the temperature to 400° F, and then select the oven cooking method.

2. Meanwhile, prepare the chicken and for this, drizzle it with oil and then sprinkle with remaining ingredients until well coated.

3. Arrange the chicken breasts on the baking pan and then bake for 35 minutes until tender.

4. Serve straight away.

NUTRITION:

- Calories: 300
- Fat: 11g
- Carbs: 0g
- Protein: 51g
- Fiber: 0g

Meat

Meatloaf

Preparation time: 10 minutes

Cooking time: 25 minutes

Servings: 4

INGREDIENTS:

- 1-pound ground beef
- 1 small white onion, peeled, chopped
- 2 medium mushrooms, sliced
- 1 tablespoon chopped thyme
- 3 tablespoons breadcrumbs
- 1 teaspoon salt
- 1/2 teaspoon ground black pepper
- 1 egg
- 1 tablespoon olive oil

DIRECTIONS:
1. Turn on the oven, set the temperature to 392 degrees F, and then select the oven cooking method.
2. Meanwhile, place beef in a large bowl, add onion, thyme, salt, black pepper, breadcrumbs, and eggs, and then stir until incorporated.
3. Spoon the beef mixture into the baking pan, smooth the top, press the mushroom slices on top and then drizzle with oil.
4. Place the pan containing prepared meatloaf into the oven and then cook for 25 minutes until the top turn nicely browned.
5. When done, let the meatloaf rest for 10 minutes, cut it into wedges, and then serve.

NUTRITION:
- Calories: 296.8
- Fat: 18.8g
- Carbs: 6g
- Protein: 24.8g
- Fiber: 0.8g

Swedish Meatballs

Preparation time: 5 minutes

Cooking time: 10 minutes

Servings: 42

INGREDIENTS:

- 8 ounces ground beef
- 1/4 of a medium white onion, peeled, grated
- 8 ounces ground pork
- 1 teaspoon salt
- 1/2 teaspoon ground black pepper
- 3/4 teaspoon ground allspice
- 2 slices of white bread
- 1 egg
- 1/2 cup milk

DIRECTIONS:

1. Turn on the oven, set the temperature to 360 degrees F, and then select the oven cooking method.
2. Meanwhile, place the bread slices in a bowl, add milk, and then let it soak for 5 minutes.
3. Then squeeze milk from the bread and tear the bread into small pieces.
4. Transfer the bread pieces into a large bowl, add beef, pork, onion, salt, black pepper, allspice, and egg and then stir until well combined.
5. Shape the mixture into small meatballs, 1 tablespoon of mixture per meatball, and then arrange the balls on a baking pan.
6. Place the baking pan into the oven and then cook the meatballs for 10 minutes until done.
7. Serve straight away.
8. Flip it and then brush the pork with half of the glaze.

9. Switch the temperature to 250 degrees, continue cooking for 10 minutes until caramelized, add remaining glaze over the pork, turn the temperature to 400 degrees F and cook for 2 minutes.
10. When done, let the pork rest for 5 minutes, cut it into slices, and then serve.

NUTRITION:

- Calories: 67
- Fat: 4.4g
- Carbs: 2.6g
- Protein: 4.2g
- Fiber: 0.1g

Pork Belly

Preparation time: 10 minutes

Cooking time: 2 hours and 30 minutes

Servings: 8

INGREDIENTS:

- 2 pounds pork belly, with skin
- 1/2 teaspoon salt
- 1/2 teaspoon ground black pepper
- 2 tablespoons olive oil

DIRECTIONS:

1. Turn on the oven, set the temperature to 350 degrees F, and then select the oven cooking method.
2. Meanwhile, prepare the pork belly and for this, make a diamond pattern across its skin by cutting through the fat and skin but not the meat.
3. Sprinkle with salt and black pepper, drizzle with oil, rub well and then place the pork skin-side up in the oven basket.

4. Cook the pork for 2 hours to 2 hours and 30 minutes until meat turns very tender, then switch the oven temperature to 425 degrees F and continue roasting for 20 minutes until the skin turns crisp.
5. When done, let the pork belly rest for 10 minutes, cut it into slices, and then serve.

NUTRITION:

- Calories: 240
- Fat: 21g
- Carbs: 0g
- Protein: 13g
- Fiber: 0g

Roast Lamb

Preparation time: 5 minutes

Cooking time: 20 minutes

Servings: 2

INGREDIENTS:

- 10 ounces lamb leg roast, butterflied
- 1 teaspoon dried rosemary
- 1 teaspoon dried thyme
- 1 tablespoon olive oil

DIRECTIONS:

1. Turn on the oven, set the temperature to 360 degrees F, and then select the oven cooking method.
2. Meanwhile, stir together thyme, rosemary, and oil until combined, and then brush this mixture generously over the lamb until coated.
3. Place the lamb leg into the oven basket and then cook for 15 to 20 minutes until cooked to desire doneness.
4. When done, cover the lamb leg with foil, let it rest for 5 minutes, and then cut it into slices.
5. Serve straight away.

NUTRITION:

- Calories: 181
- Fat: 11g
- Carbs: 1g
- Protein: 18g
- Fiber: 0g

Bread

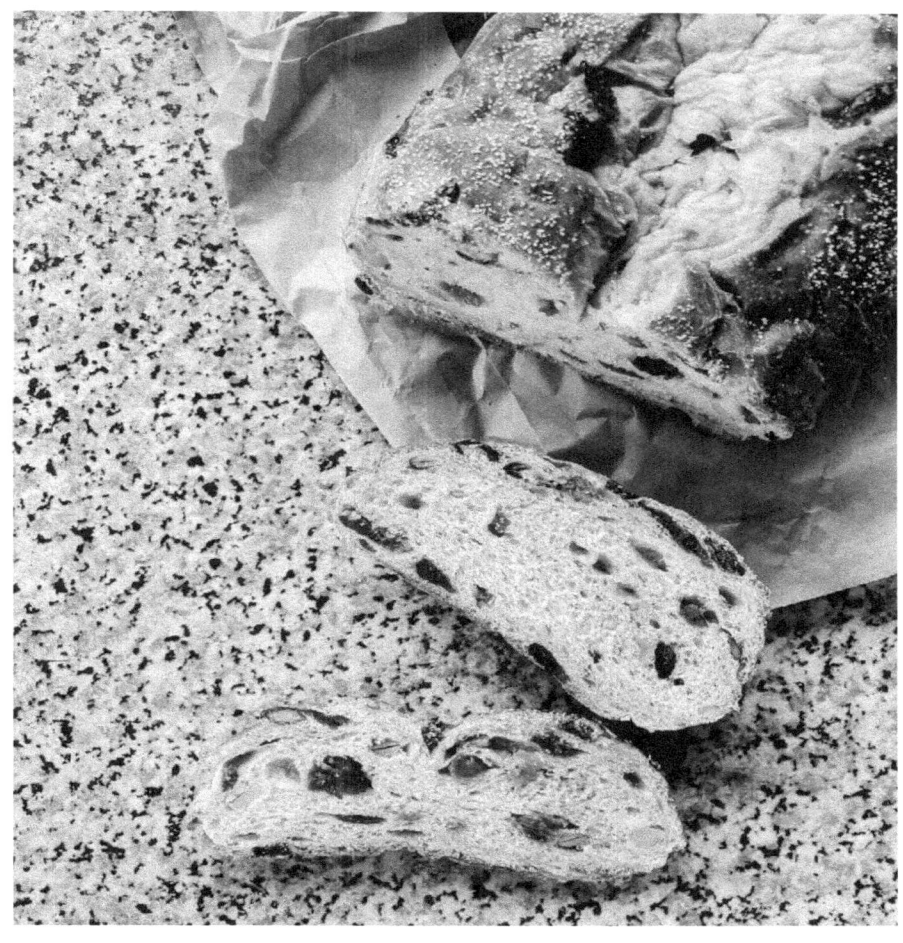

Four Cheese Margherita Pizza

Preparation time: 10 minutes

Cooking time: 30 minutes

Servings: 8

INGREDIENTS:

- 1/4 cup olive oil
- 1 tablespoon garlic, raw
- 1/2 tablespoon salt
- 8 Roma tomatoes
- 2 pizza crust
- 8 oz. mozzarella cheese
- 4 oz. fontina cheese

- 10 fresh basil
- 1/2 cup parmesan cheese, grated
- 1/2 cup feta cheese

DIRECTIONS:

1. Mix oil, garlic, and salt. Toss with tomatoes and let stand for 15 minutes.
2. Place the crust on the crisper tray and brush it with tomato marinade, then sprinkle mozzarella and fontina cheese.
3. Arrange the tomatoes on top, then sprinkle basil, parmesan cheese, and feta cheese.
4. Slide the crisper tray on shelf position 2 of the Emeril Lagasse Power oven 360 and select the pizza setting. Set the temperature at 400°F for 15 minutes. Press start.
5. Cook until the cheese is golden brown and bubbly. Repeat the cycle with the remaining pizza.
6. Serve the pizza and enjoy it.

NUTRITION:

- Calories: 551
- Carbs: 54g
- Fat: 18g
- Protein: 29g

Satay Chicken Pizza

Preparation time: 10 minutes

Cooking time: 17 minutes

Servings: 4

INGREDIENTS:

- 1 tablespoon vegetable corn oil
- 2 chicken breasts
- 4 small pita bread
- 1 cup peanut sauce
- 1 bunch spring onions
- 4 slices provolone cheese

DIRECTIONS:

1. Heat oil in a nonstick skillet and sauté the chicken for 7 minutes.
2. Spoon peanut sauce on each pita bread the sprinkle the cooked chicken. Add scallions and a slice of cheese.
3. Place the pizza on a crisper tray lined with a cookie sheet.
4. Slide the crisper tray on shelf position 2 of the Emeril Lagasse Power oven 360. Select the pizza setting. Set the temperature at 400°F for 12 minutes. Press start.
5. Let the pizza stand for 2 minutes before cutting and serving.

NUTRITION:

- Calories: 391
- Carbs: 52g
- Fat: 18g
- Protein: 7g

Black and White Pizza

Preparation time: 10 minutes

Cooking time: 20 minutes

Servings: 4

INGREDIENTS:

- 1 tablespoon olive oil
- 1/2 garlic clove, raw
- 6 oz. chicken
- 2 prepared pizza crust
- 1 cup Di Giorno Alfredo sauce
- 6 0z packed mozzarella cheese
- 1/2 cup beans
- 4 oz. jalapeno peppers
- 1 tablespoon dried parsley

DIRECTIONS:

1. Heat oil in a nonstick skillet over medium heat. Cook garlic until fragrant, then add chicken and cook until heated through.
2. Spread Alfredo sauce on the pizza crust, then sprinkle some cheese.
3. Arrange chicken strips over the cheese, then add black beans. Place peppers on top.
4. Add the remaining cheese, then garnish with parsley. Place the pizza on a crisper tray of the Emeril Lagasse Power oven 360.
5. Slide the crisper tray on shelf position 2. Select the pizza setting. Set the temperature at 450°F for 15 minutes. Press start.
6. Cook until the crust is crispy and the cheese has melted.

NUTRITION:

- Calories: 731
- Carbs: 61g
- Fat: 38g
- Protein: 41g

Bread Machine Bagels

Preparation time: 10 minutes

Cooking time: 40 minutes

Servings: 6

INGREDIENTS:

- 1 cup of water
- 1-1/2 tablespoon salt
- 2 tablespoon sugar
- 3 cups wheat flour
- 2-1/4 tablespoon yeast
- 3 tablespoon granulated sugar
- 1 tablespoon cornmeal
- 1 egg

- 3 tablespoon poppy seeds

DIRECTIONS:

1. Place water, sugar, salt, flour, and yeast in a bread machine. Select dough setting.
2. Let the dough rest on a floured surface.
3. Meanwhile, bring water to boil, then stir with sugar. Cut dough into nine pieces and roll each into a ball.
4. Flatten and poke a hole on the ball using your hands. Cover the bagels and let rest for 10 minutes.
5. Sprinkle cornmeal on a baking sheet, then transfer the bagels to boiling water. Let boil for 1 minute, then drain them on a clean paper towel.
6. Arrange the bagels on a baking sheet, then glaze them with egg and sprinkle poppy seeds.
7. Place the baking sheet on the pizza rack of the Emeril Lagasse Power oven 360 and Select the bake setting. Set the temperature at 375°F for 25 minutes. Press start.
8. The bagels should be well browned and cooked.

NUTRITION:

- Calories: 50
- Carbs: 9g
- Fat: 1.3g
- Protein: 1.4g

Bagel and Cheese Bake

Preparation time: 10 minutes

Cooking time: 50 minutes

Servings: 12

INGREDIENTS:

- 1/2 lb. bacon
- 1/2 cup onions, raw
- 3 bagels
- 1 cup cheddar cheese
- 12 eggs
- 2 cups of milk, reduced fat
- 2 tablespoon parsley
- 1/4 tablespoon black pepper
- 1/2 cup parmesan cheese, grated

DIRECTIONS:

1. Cook bacon and onion in a nonstick skillet and cook over medium heat until well browned. Drain and set aside.
2. Slice the bagel into 6 slices, then arrange them on a greased baking dish. Cover the bagels with bacon and onion mixture then top with cheese.
3. In a mixing bowl, whisk together eggs, milk, parsley, and pepper. Pour the egg mixture on the bagels and refrigerate overnight while covered.
4. Place the baking sheet on the pizza rack of the Emeril Lagasse Power oven 360 and select the bake setting. Set the temperature at 400°F for 30 minutes. Press start.
5. Sprinkle parmesan cheese and serve when warm. Enjoy.

NUTRITION:

- Calories: 249
- Carbs: 15g
- Fat: 13.5g
- Protein: 17g

Cake & Dessert

Single-Serving Chocolate Chip Cookies

Preparation time: 10 minutes

Cooking time: 8 minutes

Servings: 1

INGREDIENTS:

- 2 tablespoons butter
- 2 firmly packed tablespoons dark brown sugar
- 1 tablespoon granulated sugar
- Pinch of salt
- 1/4 teaspoon pure vanilla extract
- 1 egg yolk
- 1/4 teaspoon baking soda
- 1/4 cup all-purpose flour
- 3 heaping tablespoons semi-sweet chocolate chips

DIRECTIONS:

1. Start by preheating the toaster oven to 350°F.
2. Soften butter and combine with sugars, salt, and vanilla.
3. Add egg yolk and continue to stir.
4. Add flour and baking soda and stir until combined.
5. Add chocolate chips to bowl and mix until evenly distributed.
6. Line a pan with parchment paper and separate dough into two equal parts in pan.
7. Bake for 8 minutes.

NUTRITION:

- Calories: 667
- Sodium: 645mg
- Dietary Fiber: 3.1g
- Total Fat: 39.9g
- Total Carbs: 73.4g
- Protein: 6.2g.

Strawberry Chocolate Chip Banana Bread Bars

Preparation time: 15 minutes

Cooking time: 30 minutes

Servings: 10

INGREDIENTS:

- 1-1/4 cups white whole wheat flour
- 1 cup old-fashioned rolled oats
- 1 teaspoon ground cinnamon
- 1-1/2 teaspoons baking soda
- 2 bananas
- 1 egg
- 1/4 cup packed brown sugar
- 2 tablespoons melted coconut oil
- 3/4 cups + 1 tablespoon reduced-fat buttermilk
- 1 cup freeze-dried strawberries
- 1/4 cup semi-sweet mini chocolate chips

DIRECTIONS:

1. Start by preheating toaster oven to 350°F.
2. Combine dry ingredients in a medium bowl.
3. In a separate bowl, mash bananas and mix with egg then add brown sugar, oil, and buttermilk.
4. Combine flour mixture with banana mixture. Fold in strawberries and chocolate chips.
5. Pour batter into a greased cake pan and bake for 30 minutes. Allow to cool, then enjoy.

NUTRITION:

- Calories: 187
- Sodium: 220mg

- Dietary Fiber: 2.4g
- Total Fat: 5.4g
- Total Carbs: 31.1g
- Protein: 4.5g

Lemon Shortbread

Preparation time: 10 minutes

Cooking time: 50 minutes

Servings: 3 dozens

INGREDIENTS:

- 2 cups all-purpose flour
- 1 1/4 teaspoons coarse salt
- 2 cup of unsalted butter
- 5 teaspoons finely grated lemon zest
- 1 tablespoon fresh lemon juice
- 3/4 cup confectioners' sugar

DIRECTIONS:

1. Preheat oven to 300°, with rack in the upper third. Filter flour and salt into a bowl; put in a safe spot. Put one cup of the butter into the bowl of an electric mixer fitted with the paddle attachment. Blend on medium-fast until it is fluffy, 3 to 5 mins, scratching disadvantages of the bowl. Progressively add sugar; beat until pale and soft, around 2 mins. Blend in lemon zing and juice.
2. Decrease in speed to low. Add flour blend at the same time; blend until just consolidated.
3. Divide batter, and shape into plates. Wrap each in plastic, and refrigerate 60 mins.
4. Working with 1 plate at a time, roll out the batter on a daintily floured surface to 1/4 inch thick. Cut out rounds with a 2-inch fluted shaper. Space 1 inch separated on baking sheets fixed with parchment. Refrigerate 30 mins.
5. Bake until pale golden brown, 22 to 25 mins. Move treats to a wire rack; let cool totally. Residue with confectioners' sugar.

NUTRITION:

- Calories: 145
- Carbs: 3.6g
- Protein: 2.1g
- Fat: 13.6g

Carrot Cake Cookies

Preparation time: 10 minutes

Cooking time: 15 minutes

Servings: 24 cookies

INGREDIENTS:

- 1/4 cup brown sugar
- 1/4 cup vegetable oil
- 1/2 teaspoon baking soda
- 1/4 cup applesauce or fruit puree
- 1/4 teaspoon nutmeg
- 1 egg
- 1/2 teaspoon vanilla
- 1/2 cup flour
- 1/2 cup wheat flour
- 1/2 teaspoon baking powder
- A dash of salt
- 1/2 teaspoon ground cinnamon
- 1/4 teaspoon ground ginger
- 1 cup old-fashioned rolled oats
- 3/4 cup grated carrots
- 1/2 cup raisins or golden raisins

DIRECTIONS:

1. In a large mixing bowl combine together sugar, oil, applesauce, egg and vanilla.
2. In another bowl, mix all dry ingredients. Then, add dry ingredients to wet ingredients. Mix till blended. Toss in carrots and raisins.
3. Drop by teaspoonful onto silicone baking ring or parchment-lined cookie sheet.

4. Place on 1-inch rack and cook at 300 degrees F (Level 8) for 12-14 minutes or until golden brown.

NUTRITION:

- Calories: 252
- Carbs: 20g
- Total Fat: 7g
- Protein: 3g

Homemade Fudgy Brownies

Preparation time: 10 minutes

Cooking time: 50 minutes

Servings: 10

INGREDIENTS:

- 3/4 cup butter salted or unsalted
- 1 3/4 cup dark chocolate chips divided into the recipe
- 1 teaspoon espresso powder optional
- 3/4 teaspoon sea salt
- 1 1/2 cups sugar
- 5 large eggs
- 1/3 cup vegetable oil
- 2 teaspoon vanilla extract
- 1/2 cup of unsweetened cocoa powder
- 1 1/2 cups flour all-purpose

DIRECTIONS:

1. Cut the butter into a little slice and add to the oven Cold and Hot Blender. Add 1 cup of the chocolate chips. Put the cover on the blender and select cook mode on high. Cook for 3 mins, at that point, beat a few times, and turn the warmth down to low. Scratch the sides if necessary. Cook on low for 2 additional mins. Include 1 tsp coffee powder. Heartbeat until smooth.
2. Add the salt and sugar, press the beat button for around 5 seconds. Add the eggs, oil, and vanilla concentrate. Press the beat button for around 5 seconds. Scratch down the sides. Ensure the Batter is all around fused, beat again if necessary.
3. Sift the flour and the cocoa powder prior to adding to the blender. Add the combination in 1/4-1/2 cup increases, beat for around 5 seconds between every option. Or then again you can utilize the low mix work. On the off chance that there is remaining flour on top, utilize the alter device or a spatula to push it down into the blender. You may need to mix the hitter to fuse the last expansion of flour/cocoa powder. Utilize the low mix setting to wrapping up joining the hitter. Scratch down the sides.
4. Once all the flour/cocoa powder is fused, include the excess 3/4 cup of chocolate chips and mix with a spatula.
5. Line an 11.5"X 9" with one or the other parchment or a Silpat. In the case of utilizing parchment paper, cover the lower part of the container with Butter or Crisco prior to putting the parchment on the dish.
6. Pour the brownie hitter into the readied container and spot it on the rack in the oven. Set the baking work on 325°F for 35 mins. Eliminate and let cool for at any rate 15 mins. Cut and serve!

NUTRITION:

- Calories: 145
- Carbs: 3.6g
- Protein: 2.1g
- Fat: 13.6g

Teriyaki Sauce

Preparation time: 10 minutes

Cooking time: 30 minutes

Servings: 12

INGREDIENTS:

- 1/2 cup soy sauce
- 1/4 cup brown sugar
- See brown sugar alternative (for low sugar option)
- 1 1/2 teaspoons fresh ginger, minced
- 1 teaspoon garlic, minced
- 1 tablespoon honey (Vegans: use agave honey or sweetener of choice)
- 1 teaspoon sesame oil
- 3 tablespoons mirin (see note)
- 1/4 cup water mixed with 3 teaspoons cornstarch

DIRECTIONS:

1. Join all ingredients in a little pan, heat to the point of boiling lessen warmth, and stew for around 4 mins. Eliminate or remove from warmth and let cool.
2. It can be preserved in the refrigerator for just 7 days. Makes around 1/4 cups teriyaki sauce.

NOTE: If utilizing as a marinade, overlook the cornstarch and let the sauce cool totally prior to utilizing.

NUTRITION:

- Calories: 145
- Carbs: 3.6g
- Protein: 2.1g
- Fat: 13.6g

Poppy Seed Pound Cake

Preparation time: 10 minutes

Cooking time: 20 minutes

Servings: 8

INGREDIENTS:

- 2 large eggs
- 1/2 cup coconut milk
- 1/3 cup unsalted butter
- 1/4 teaspoon vanilla extract
- 2 tablespoons psyllium husk powder
- 1 1/2 teaspoons baking powder
- 2 tablespoons poppy seeds
- 1 1/2 cup almond flour

DIRECTIONS:

1. Preheat the oven for 5 minutes.

2. In a mixing bowl, combine all ingredients.
3. Use a hand mixer to mix everything.
4. Pour into a small loaf pan that will fit in the oven.
5. Bake for 20 minutes at 3750 F or until a toothpick inserted in the middle comes out clean.

NUTRITION:

- Calories: 145
- Carbs: 3.6g
- Protein: 2.1g
- Fat: 13.6g

Apple-Toffee Upside-Down Cake

Preparation time: 10 minutes

Cooking time: 30 minutes

Servings: 9

INGREDIENTS:

- 1/4 cup almond butter
- 1/4 cup sunflower oil
- 1/2 cup chopped walnuts
- 1 cup coconut sugar
- 3/4 cup water
- 1 1/2 teaspoons mixed spice
- 1 cup plain flour
- 1 lemon zest
- 1 teaspoon baking soda
- 1 teaspoon vinegar
- 3 apples, cored and sliced

DIRECTIONS:

1. Preheat the oven to 3900 F.
2. In a skillet, melt the almond butter and 3 tablespoons of sugar. Pour mixture over a baking dish that will fit in the oven. Arrange the slices of apples on top. Set aside.
3. In a mixing bowl, combine flour, 3/4 cup sugar, and baking soda. Add the mixed spice.
4. In another bowl, mix the oil, water, vinegar, and lemon zest. Stir in the chopped walnuts.
5. Combine the wet ingredients to dry ingredients until well combined.
6. Pour over the tin with apple slices.
7. Leave to cook for 30 minutes.

NUTRITION:

- Calories: 145
- Carbs: 3.6g
- Protein: 2.1g
- Fat: 13.6g

Chocolate Nut Brownies

Preparation time: 5 minutes

Cooking time: 30 minutes

Servings: 12

INGREDIENTS:

- 1/2 cup unsalted butter
- 2 ounces unsweetened chocolate
- 1 cup sugar
- 2 eggs
- 1 teaspoon vanilla
- 2/3 cup all-purpose, unbleached flour
- 1/2 cup chopped nuts (I used walnuts)
- 1/2 teaspoon baking powder (Decrease to 1/4 teaspoon for high altitude)
- 1/4 teaspoon salt

DIRECTIONS:

1. Heat oven to 350 degrees.
2. Grease (with butter) and lightly flour bottom only of 8 or 9-inch square pan.
3. In a large saucepan, melt butter and chocolate over low heat, stirring constantly. Remove from heat; cool slightly.
4. Blend in sugar. Beat in eggs, one at a time. Stir in remaining ingredients.
5. Spread in prepared pan. Bake at 350 degrees for 25 to 30 minutes or until set in the center. Be sure not to overbake if you want a softer center.
6. Remove from oven and cool completely on a wire rack. Cut into bars to serve.

NUTRITION:

- Calories: 181
- Fat: 13g
- Fiber: 2g
- Carbs: 4g
- Protein: 5g

Measurement Conversion Chart

Term	Abbreviation	Nationality	Dry or liquid	Metric equivalent	Equivalent in context
American and British Variances					
cup	c., C.		usually liquid	237 milliliters	16 tablespoons or 8 ounces
ounce	fl oz, fl. oz.	American	liquid only	29.57 milliliters	
		British	either	28.41 milliliters	
gallon	gal.	American	liquid only	3.785 liters	4 quarts
		British	either	4.546 liters	4 quarts
inch	in, in.			2.54 centimeters	
ounce	oz, oz.	American	dry	28.35 grams	1/16 pound
			liquid	see OUNCE	see OUNCE
pint	p., pt.	American	liquid	0.473 liter	1/8 gallon or 16 ounces
			dry	0.551 liter	1/2 quart
		British	either	0.568 liter	
pound	lb.		dry	453.592 grams	16 ounces
Quart	q., qt, qt.	American	liquid	0.946 liter	1/4 gallon or 32 ounces
			dry	1.101 liters	2 pints
		British	either	1.136 liters	
Teaspoon	t., tsp., tsp		either	about 5 milliliters	1/3 tablespoon
Tablespoon	T., tbs., tbsp.		either	about 15 milliliters	3 teaspoons or 1/2 ounce

Volume (Liquid)

American Standard (Cups & Quarts)	American Standard (Ounces)	Metric (Milliliters & Liters)
2 tbsp.	1 fl. oz.	30 ml
1/4 cup	2 fl. oz.	60 ml
1/2 cup	4 fl. oz.	125 ml
1 cup	8 fl. oz.	250 ml
1 1/2 cups	12 fl. oz.	375 ml
2 cups or 1 pint	16 fl. oz.	500 ml
4 cups or 1 quart	32 fl. oz.	1000 ml or 1 liter
1 gallon	128 fl. oz.	4 liters

Volume (Dry)

American Standard	Metric
1/8 teaspoon	5 ml
1/4 teaspoon	1 ml
1/2 teaspoon	2 ml
3/4 teaspoon	4 ml
1 teaspoon	5 ml
1 tablespoon	15 ml
1/4 cup	59 ml
1/3 cup	79 ml
1/2 cup	118 ml
2/3 cup	158 ml
3/4 cup	177 ml
1 cup	225 ml
2 cups or 1 pint	450 ml
3 cups	675 ml
4 cups or 1 quart	1 liter
1/2 gallon	2 liters
1 gallon	4 liters

Dry Measure Equivalents

3 teaspoons	1 tablespoon	1/2 ounce	14.3 grams
2 tablespoons	1/8 cup	1 ounce	28.3 grams
4 tablespoons	1/4 cup	2 ounces	56.7 grams
5 1/3 tablespoons	1/3 cup	2.6 ounces	75.6 grams
8 tablespoons	1/2 cup	4 ounces	113.4 grams
12 tablespoons	3/4 cup	6 ounces	.375 pound
32 tablespoons	2 cups	16 ounces	1 pound

Oven Temperatures

American Standard	Metric
250° F	130° C
300° F	150° C
350° F	180° C
400° F	200° C
450° F	230° C

Weight (Mass)

American Standard (Ounces)	Metric (Grams)
1/2 ounce	15 grams
1 ounce	30 grams
3 ounces	85 grams
3.75 ounces	100 grams
4 ounces	115 grams
8 ounces	225 grams
12 ounces	340 grams
16 ounces or 1 pound	450 grams

www.ingramcontent.com/pod-product-compliance
Lightning Source LLC
Chambersburg PA
CBHW070929080526
44589CB00013B/1445